Does She Have a Name?

Also by George Witte

Deniability

The Apparitioners

Does She Have a Name?

Poems

George Witte

NYQ Books™

The New York Quarterly Foundation, Inc.
New York, New York

NYQ Books™ is an imprint of The New York Quarterly Foundation, Inc.

The New York Quarterly Foundation, Inc.
P. O. Box 2015
Old Chelsea Station
New York, NY 10113

www.nyq.org

Copyright © 2014 by George Witte

First Edition

Set in New Baskerville

Layout and Design by Raymond P. Hammond
Cover Photo by George Witte

Library of Congress Control Number: 2014931065

ISBN: 978-1-63045-001-4

Does She Have a Name?

Acknowledgments

Thanks to the editors of these journals for first publishing certain poems in this collection:

32 Poems: What's Wrong With You
Able Muse: Exit Line
Antioch Review: The Dragon
Kin: More; Names to Faces, Faces to Names
Map Literary: Revenants
Measure: Atlas
New South: If I Should Die; Standard of Care; The Defender
Ploughshares: Does She Have a Name?
Nimrod: Brightening Glance
Raintown Review: The Stolen Girl
Southwest Review: Consonance; Do Not Resuscitate
Virginia Quarterly Review: The Blister
Yale Review: Mr. Nobody

Contents

for Kris and Helen

Does She Have a Name?

Does She Have a Name?

The intern's wand assayed your abdomen
with soundwaves   dowsing the nocturnal pool
she swam within   pale cave dweller   tipped down
to pass between existences   asleep
forehead globed beneath her body's question
There she is   Everything's okay   except
the blood   a sudden flux enriched your gown
tear in the placental wall   *Nothing wrong*
the intern said   no sign of fetal stress
no reason to disturb the resident
who slept until his presence was required
your labor quickened   *Progressing nicely*
the intern mumbled under breath   then left
you to progress   bleeding out   unaware
how close death brushed   our cells a poisoned fruit
the cure expulsion or delivery
whatever's first   the monitors conferred
in secret tongues   regarding fetal heart
and lungs   the intern strode in   discomposed
by mystery   her printout bucketing
you felt the urge to urinate   sat up
and at that moment the placenta ripped
abrupted   peeled away   the intern burst
your sac to fix a lead into her skull
your water gushed rust brown   the lead relayed
a thready beat that flickered out   flatlined
one nurse slammed a hand against the desk call
She's going brady get him in here now
and so the resident emerged   blinking
in fluorescence   confused   torn raw from dream's
nutritious tissue   she drowned inside you
while he scrubbed   counting minutes to himself
the anesthesia pulled you under   *Now*
he cut   digging through your ravaged garden
then lifted her   our daughter   limp and blue
while you lay gutted   sewn in senselessness

15

the NICU team convened its ministry
a laying on of hands and oxygen
revived her from baptism into breath
one asked me for her name   to humanize
the sum of their procedure   revenant
in limbo   comatose   alive   *Helen*

29 Minutes

Prime
time: Time
enough to drown,
drift between that world
and this, wander neither/nor alone.
No glowing welcome host of ancestors
who shy away, reject your tourist status.
Not quite time to enter other lives, begin
again as seed, translucent fertile egg, divide and multiply
or be erased, devoured to dust, compressed in stone, burned
for heat to make or move. Time enough for death,
cool draft insinuating through the room—*just looking, thanks*—
to pause before the NICU team's intense ablution
of your corpse, then move away, dispossessed
by breath. You breathe. A hush
suspends us, witnessing this second
birth: Flush with oxygen,
your journey done,
arriving in
time.

Do Not Resuscitate

Machines attend your body's winding down,
pitiless recorders: Blood oxygen
declines, respirations slow and shallow,
pulse a thread your nervous heart unravels.
The protocol's to manage this event,
ensure the hospital is paid what rent
we owe for entering its underground.
The bed, the curtained cubicle surround
our family, soon to be diminished,
these days together marked by tests you failed,
Apgar, hearing, the brain's electric yield.
The unit doctors counsel paperwork
absolving them and us: *It's for the best,
you're young enough to have another one.*
We sign the DNR and get a kit,
brochures of funeral homes and florists,
bottom feeders gluttoning on discards.
You're written off; there's nothing to be done.

We hold your hands and say your ancient name,
once cause for war to regain property,
in our time pedigree of aged aunts.
Your levels pause above the danger zone
as if you hear and turn to follow us—
familiar voices, abandoned whispers—
though where we lead and what we promise you's
ambiguous at best. The monitor
unscrolls its analytic lullaby.
You choose to be what we would not abide.

Standard of Care

This time we know   no guarantees
intelligence won't save our skins
or hers   we'll whisper *pretty please*
rend hair and blacken eyes   bargain
years against her safe arrival
we'll daven   beg   consult the star-
cast calendars   burn animals
to ease economies of scale
sing praise until throats spatter blood
our evidence   this time she'll wail
alive   flushed pink with oxygen
not blue   not comatose   machines
won't incubate her   cradled in
a humming hive of wire so frail
we couldn't disentangle her
to hold   but laid on hands   caressed
her name in case she hung upon
the syllables undrowned   too late
we understood how rough love is
revisited each minute's toll
we could have   should have   didn't   done
we get it now   the consequence
we won't expect again   this time

Mom's Iguana

A regal exile to our neighborhood
Jerry languished on her shoulder's transept.
Discoloring with warm or cooler blood,
collar fringed, claws meticulously kept,

it toured the house. She'd vacuum, wash, prepare
three meals devoured before she sat, domain
invisible to those who didn't care
enough to wonder what she wouldn't deign

to say. Arrayed in alien disguise
she greeted gossips out for daily bread,
politely parried inquiries and lies
with smiling innocence until they fled

the lizard's curled exploratory tongue.
Though mine, it knew who fed and watered us;
when lifted from the rank terrarium
impaled my skin and twisted furious

until she stroked its throat with fingertips
exquisitely assured and murmured sounds
my dictionary didn't list. Its grip
relaxed. From each of twenty puncture wounds

blood welled a bead. She felt my brow—"You're hot"—
unfurling it at ease from tennis wrist
to scapula. "He smells your fear: So what.
If people sniff you out they're merciless."

It died undignified, by slow degrees,
cooked atop a bathroom radiator.
She flushed it down, "That's that" for elegy,
my punishment to scour its remnant gore,

then sat alone, one cigarette enough,
smoke softening the glare of providence,
surrounded by her comfortable stuff,
and asked me not to interrupt, this once.

Mutterance

She kept opinion under breath
behind a smile exhaling smoke,
teeth bared, polite, impolitic.
Rehearsing lines best left unsaid
by wives in comfortable homes
she'd sheathe her whetted tongue, bite lips
white against temptation's whisper,
pare nails, shave legs and underarms,
tease out and tweeze embedded hair.
From luncheons, doubles, PTA,
a fourth for golf or evening bridge,
companionable but apart,
she sought an exile's library
and nestled there content, our cat
her telepathic confidante,
impassive, sly, entwining legs,
eyes widened as if mesmerized
by words too keen for human ears.
If the shoe fits…when the shit hits…
You perfect people want my life
well you can have it. Overheard
by eavesdroppers or passersby
she'd hush, mysteriously shy,
a girl inside the sibyl's rind,
then mutter *Nothing. Never mind.*

Atlas

Face down upon the kitchen floor you lick
linoleum and scattered coffee grounds
for comfort, sustenance against panic.

Remember movie seats with Sensurround?—
heart vibrating, breath amplified in rasps,
voice enormous but unheard. No sound,

no witnesses; the phone's beyond your grasp.
Post-stroke, you practiced this for hours alone:
Assemble balance on one leg, collapse.

Again. Again. Arise or lie undone,
piss-damp, face slick with snot and blood and tears,
incoherent with humiliation.

Wedge hand and knee for leverage, then tear
from earth and shoulder up the weight of air.

Recreation

Before the circus, Dad belayed
us underneath the delicate
machinery of rope and wire
to pitch amusements, corridors
where freaks displayed their qualities.
Prone, impassive in squat cages
smelling of ammonia and shit,
they stood attentive only when
sufficient audience had paused.
Decades since, Dad's precisely on,
passing swift through practiced changes
he contorts a face or hobbles
howling vacant-eyed: The giant's
mute pleas for popcorn or release;
the midget snarling comic taunts,
fine hands corded tough with muscle
when they flexed; dull animals, plus
or minus parts, their misery
worth the ticket price. Last and best,
not jailed but on a pedestal
of sorts, draped cleverly so we
beheld full upper arms and thighs,
a woman. Her laughter's music
summoned *Closer* to her harbor,
shoals and folds where flesh protruded
from the gown, pale Charybdis,
throat extended like a swan's
to call and summon back the song
from her forgetful acolytes,
who laughed until the tone declined
one half-note to a minor key
where merriment became the edge
of rage, a rasp that sawed our fun
off at the knees and made us hush.

We leaned to hear; contemptuous,
she turned away and tucked her head.
Now she animates our house, Dad's
recreation—too loud, we fear
the neighbors will look in at us.
There's one thing they've got over me,
Mom says. *Remember: They got paid.*

Eagle Eye

The mall she once bestrode
defeats her now, vast ziggurat
where entrances and levels lead astray,

by strokes erased, slick halls
impossible to navigate.
One hand maneuvering the wheel she parks

ten limping minutes off,
dismissible by passersby,
suburban crone: Gone prematurely white,

a grimace baring teeth
clenched brown upon her cigarette,
propped up on tripod cane and brace, alone.

A shopper tallies spoils
within the space marked Handicapped,
brazenly adept, tennis-fit and tan.

Entitled, after all,
time being what it is, she turns.
"What the fuck you looking at?" Drawing down

her Merit, glowing tip
a wand deployed for emphasis,
Mom measures head to toe and back again

and leisurely exhales.
"Not much." Impeccable blue eyes
divining secret deficits she lifts

one cool, inquiring brow.
The woman gasps and staggers back,
spilled bags in disarray while close above

a shadow vectors down,
pinions spread to slow momentum,
then veers away, not merciful but bored,

conserving energy
to seek more worthy prey. Point made,
Mom politely bows, going on her way.

The Healers

She lays the arm along the tabletop.
Cool meat, nerves severed at the brain. One hand
unfolds the other's fingers, wedding band
embedded on the swollen joint, nails cropped.
Her doctor says massage relaxes tone,
perhaps awakens muscle memory.
Down tips to wrist she summons by degree
reluctant life from brittle skin and bone
as we, despairing, slather you in oil
the therapist supplied with calm advice,
and rub your infant limbs, a sacrifice
to gods malignant and irrational.
You smile reflexively as if amused
by good intentions, helpless to refuse.

Spouse and Issue

In this my will and testament I leave
all worldly goods to spouse, through you to her,
in complicated trust we can't conceive
without the tax attorney's sinecure
and bill. She's one, our salvaged miracle,
her life a file of specialists' reports,
each scan and MRI an oracle
portending nothing: No flaw, no surge short-
circuiting her brain, no apparent *why*.
We budget urgent care and special needs,
ensure sufficient income should we die
together or, divorced, succumb to greed.
Asleep, our issue shudders in your arms.
I sign in triplicate against more harm.

Kind

A pause. It's coming. Silent in suspense
we kneel before your rocking chair, observant,
pencils poised to reckon time and symptom.
The seizure flows, possessing us. Each jolt
clamps unannounced, disfiguring your brow:
Grimace, shoulder shrug, chin thrust left and down.
Shudder as if gripped by bone-cold talons.
No lapse in consciousness or self-control.
A staring spell, Eurydice in thrall,
pillar-stiff until we gently coax, call
you back to our defenseless realm: *Helen!*

We learn the alphabet of acronyms:
CATSCAN, MRI, sleeping EEG.
Neurologists agree to disagree,
arrange new tests but never diagnose.
If it walks like a duck and quacks like a duck
one doctor says and shrugs with palms upraised,
persuading us to medicate and see.
Curing you is murderous; your liver's
spoiled, drains and brushes clog with baby hair.
Like plugging leaks with tape and softened wax
we barter Depakote for Topamax.
Embattled meals require a force-fed pill.
We hold you down and stroke your throat, until
the swallow reflex overwhelms the gag.
You counter by refusing food so ribs
protrude in struts beneath your jaundiced skin.

In time the seizures lighten, burn away
like morning fog above this quiet lake
we stare into, aged faces joined in yours,
first vacation calming months of panic.
You laugh and splash reflection into shards;
grey water smoothes us whole, a family.
Then from nowhere and behind our sight line
vectors arrow past: A flock of ducks crash-
settles in one body, surrounding us.
Watchful but unafraid, they circle close
to plunder shallow weeds, then turn away,
confide in who knows what pre-lingual tongue
of clicks and furtive coded vocalogues,
and when you flap and shriek delight
release with wingbeat froth, exploding up
to thrum above our echoed squawks goodbye,
toward a landing place, among their kind.

Charity

Admission paid to someone's gracious house
we're knowingly appraised as parents of.
Their names stop conversation, furrow brows;
everyone's polite, smiles engraved above

crisp crudités we grateful beggars choose,
ashamed our hunger shows. The kinder moms
mime sympathy, ambitious ones excuse
themselves to stalk the bar and bathroom scrum

for prodigies to pit their own against.
It's our privilege to be patronized.
Uncharitably disobedient
we laugh and roll exaggerated eyes,

then bargain playdates for our miscast kids—
runts and autists, delayed, disordered, halt—
recite encoded acronyms of dread
like pleas from cowed believers' knees: *Our fault,*

our father who, forgive our trespasses
as we forgive, deliver us from this.

The Dragon

Your nightguest comes in clotted ripping coughs,
  old smoker's emphysema wheeze.
    Afraid, I know enough
  to carry you outside and ease
stiff lungs with humid evening air, admire
  this star or that, pretend we're blessed
    as others say we are.
  Your life depends on Orapred,
Flovent and Albuterol, medicines
  assuaging raw alveoli.
    I cradle you against
  congestion, lullaby a lie,
slow time to hasten you asleep. You breathe;
  chest falls and rises, oxygen
    plumps blue lips red. Beneath
  my palm your heart: *Again. Again.*

Brightening Glance

The gym's ball-light cast silhouettes,
blue stars that swarmed the stage, then disappeared.
In scarlet caps and snowflake wings
your class lined up, obedient, to sing.
Brain numbed by Phenobarbital
you could not shape stiff mouth and tongue to speech,
struck dumb by seizure's afterburn.
We wondered if you knew why consonants
required such practice, /s/ and /f/
surmised by reading others' lips and hands
but rarely heard, that register
destroyed before you even woke from birth's
abruption, drowned by protocol.

Clutching hands, we imagined your unease.
The song began; you stood alone,
small and stunned, frozen in our hopeful gaze
like some nocturnal animal
surprised by morning light. And then you ran,
stage front and center—electric
sneakers flashing out their coded firefly
language—to gallop a ballet,
eyes searching for us in that darkened crowd,
their glint defiant and alive.
We laughed and wept, now understood: You knew,
you'd thought it through, in secret glee
rehearsed your dance, and in such dancing, sang.

The Stolen Girl

I overhear you educating dolls
arranged attentively in rows, soft voice
assuming every part and pitch to tell
the monkey's pranks, the ballerina's dreams.
We muddled through your stillborn sacrifice
for hospital insurance premiums:
Hearing compromised, brain's electrics prone
to short, balance skewed and speech expedient,
rough alphabet of grimaces and groans.
With you we learned how effortful life is
when human grants are lost, your sleeping rent
by dream or seizure extricating cries
as payment due from wayward revenants
like you, who'd trespassed in a blackened realm.
Some found in you confirming evidence
of prayer's power; others backed away,
indifferent listeners or overwhelmed
by death in life's array. Through therapy
each hard-won consonant and vowel built
a language from reluctant lips and tongue
until the fairy tale affliction—guilt
that silenced children for their parents' sins—
began to lift, like fog beneath new sun.
First signs, then words combined in sentences.
Now clocks align, the calendar unfurls
with names of friends, not specialists,
your book describes a recollected world
of wickedness and guile where witches rage,
the stolen girl they'd cursed to limbo kissed
awake, seeming unaware of damage.

By Heart

Which lullabies attend your wane,
which stories calm or nightmare-fill,
which drugs suppress electrical
malfunctionings that seize your brain—

The warning label side effects
measured out by trial and error,
trading benefits for terror,
short term for permanent defects—

Ours the burden of decisions
made in grief, ours mistrustful hope,
our love a gleaming microscope
of scrutiny you swim within—

Our vision clouds, then clarifies
with tears you watch us wipe away,
curious, alert: *What are they?*
One day we'll abdicate the lies

you learn by heart; abashed, confess
how death's dry tongue caressed your name.
Until then we defer the blame:
They're how the eyes show happiness.

If I Should Die

Two tables, each a charnel boat or bier
to ferry bodies dredged ashore.
Your doctor sewed his carve and left, ashamed;
the room stank like a slaughterhouse.
Gassed and hollowed out, gown hem damp with blood,
you slept through her resurrection—
no miracle, but technician's labor.
A voice tolled minutes: *Twelve Fifteen*
beyond which life was not desirable.
Hauling back her vital functions,
breath and pulse and nervous reflex, the team
surrounded her, blue sacrifice
machines surveyed and cast their spell upon,
then hissed. *She's breathing,* someone said.
But we didn't do you any favors.

Years later, rowing her to sleep,
our lullaby routine no longer soothes.
Fighting ease, thrashing side to side
a bedtime fable frightens her to ask
if you will die, if I, if she....
We answer by evasion, bargain time
against the day such knowledge brings.
What invades her dreams, pricking her to cry?
Does Sleeping Beauty terrify
because the princess lingers comatose,
or is her second waking worse—
the ruined kingdom overgrown, the prince
fluorescent as a surgeon come
to kiss and claim her firstborn memory?

Revenants

Hair hennaed to a martial tease,
left arm and leg dead weight, brain seared
by errant surgery and strokes
you mangle social niceties,
harangue off-key, laugh late at jokes
old friends find inappropriate.
Your garden flourishes and sours
untended, rampant in neglect.
Rose arbors buckle under thorns;
the Women's Club no longer tours.
Couch pocked with burns from cigarettes
set down while nodding off you read
contemplatively—no regrets.
Murdered wives, suburban nightmares,
kids exiled to their predators
in wooded lots or storage sheds,
cast under spell, preserved in thrall
until awakened with a kiss.
Satisfied, you close the lurid
thing, gleaming like a casket lid.
"These people must be idiots.
Since when does money guarantee
release? Nothing's automatic.
Funny: they all believe in God."

Your granddaughter tunes in and out,
hearing aids abuzz with static.
She's culled your girlhood library
from boxes marked Don't Throw Away:
Reader's Digest *Iliad*,
Alice, Mowgli, first-edition *Oz*,
Little House and *Little Women*.
Misshapen hobbled words emerge
through awkward lips and tongue, her brain
short-circuited by voltage surge
like yours, outriders freezer burned

between that sunless world and this.
You scrutinize her head to toe,
a pro appraising deficits
beneath her hearing, under breath.
"Those doctors really fucked you up."
She nods to hide confusion. "Huh?"
You smile as if to reassure—
too wide, she flinches back in fear,
the mirror image strange, undone
but recognizable from long
ago, familiar passerby
accosted with her given name
who stops, aghast, then turns away.

Exit Line

Beneath each thunk and hiss of oxygen
the a.c. hummed the shade-drawn bedroom cool.
Inside her paper skin cells multiplied
and fed; she dripped dark honey tinged with blood,
clouding bags of bladder bile and urine.
To let her smoke we'd unplug the machine,
strip tape from cheeks and pull out nostril tubes,
lift her powdered, moistened, morphined ruin
from bed to chair, then wheel her where the view
regarded roses and perennials.
Hacking every puff she craved such pleasure,
absolved from disapproving glares, her death
permission to ignite these stolen breaths,
mind her business and damn all consequence.

No cards revealed, no last-gasp common sense,
no pleas to God—she didn't take that pill—
nothing left to ask about or answer.
She'd grimace thanks for water on her lips,
apologize when turned to bandage sores,
polite, composed, small mercies no excuse
for blubbering or gab. Long muscles flensed,
bones abrading skin, she refused all food
and settled in to starve this chrysalis.
Dying offended her intelligence,
task fulfilled like church or social function,
bullshit piety and chitchat wasting
time she couldn't borrow. Fed up, bored stiff,
she said to no one in particular
I've had enough, let's get this over with.

Mr. Nobody

Who swilled the milk except its dregs,
savored coffee and unpeeled
the final fragrant pear,
left cereal crumbs, dry loaf heels,
ice cream's rimed and rheumy corners,
one cracked egg?

Who didn't dump the trash until
it stank, then jammed the bag to split
so rinds and grounds and skins and shells
required a housewife's genuflection,
hands and knees against the stain
that would not lift?

Who soured our wine to vinegar,
chewed cheese and crackers on the loveseat's
discontinued fabric? Whose embers
charred the oriental, whose beer wept
its mute, mysterious initial
into the antique sidetable?

The bed unmade,
the toilet smeared,
the drain hair-clogged, the laundry rotten,
the floors not swept or mopped,
whatever's half-done or forgotten—
who's the first to notice and complain?

Whose face did she intuit,
having posed these questions
for amusement's sake, watched
beyond peripheries, listened under breath,
smelled burning out of reach,
glimpsed but never saw? And as she died,

tongue jutting in and out between parched lips
in muscle memory of speech,
who knelt with us in that darkened room,
too powerful to be named,
and lingered silent, silencing
on its extended tip?

Night Moth

In your wake the usual detritus:
Half-smoked cigarettes, pages folded down,
brushes shedding silver hair, empty bras.
Here and there we witness visitation,
a closet open, air displacing air
received with *hmmms*, an eyebrow raised. No one's
lingered comatose, limp and unaware,
or crossed the borderline from is to was
but Helen, four, who drowned while being born,
29 minutes without oxygen
until she breathed. She knows that other world,
imagines you transforming in cocoon,
new limbs and abdomen, damp wings unfurled
to soar beneath anthropomorphic moons.

More

A graph aligning hertz and decibel.
A shell, conducting sound from minute bones
precisely calibrated to transmit
compression waves through cilia so frail
the follicles eroded, oxygen-
deprived at birth. Your audiologist
inscribes a speech banana on the grid.
Ambiguous half-smile of normal range
within which frequency and volume mesh,
the precious ground your hearing occupies
is riven by a downward sloping line
that trails away, a map of compromise
recording all you cannot hear to say.
Age three, you grunt and squawk, half-animal,
mime "milk" with udder tugs, tap fingertips
on lips for baby food you still devour,
tuck thumb between forefingers to request
another diaper change. Your therapist
goads speech with physical release, intense
encounters face to face three weekly hours.
Cross-legged on the floor she conjures noise;
you bellow, mouth distended, jaw adrift.
Rough consonants and vowels rise unbound,
extruded one by one, each phoneme freed
from long confinement into air and light.
You squat and stand as if supporting weight,
windmill frantic arms to force this flower:
"Mo-." Another try, fists clenched, beginning
shoulder-high, plunged down, around, and up. *"More!"*
Within the darkened observation room
I weep; the one-way window's secrecy
admits your stare, triumphantly aware.
You heard yourself and know I did, that word
a door you shoulder open, and go out.

What's Wrong With You

You chew lank hair until it's frayed
in clumps no comb can disembraid.

Eat sloppily so ketchup gores
your lips, school clothes, the just-cleaned floor

we make you sponge and disinfect.
Stain panties with ungoverned shit.

Aren't deaf enough to recompense,
can't sue your doctors' negligence

for seizure lightning, childhood lost,
speech gagged to save insurance costs.

Run headlong into trees, collide
with doors and tables' undersides,

each flight of stairs portending harm.
Scab-kneed and bloody-nosed, stiff arm

through glass as if it isn't there,
astonished by the taloned air,

shrieking not from pain but conscience
pricked to fear our disappointments.

Sneeze gouts of snot and spit despite
requests to be considerate,

then weep when disciplined with threats—
friends lost or never made, classmates

sickened, time-outs and no T.V.—
until you beg: *Do you love me?*

That's not the point; of course we do.
You need to learn what others know,

practice what makes people people.
If we don't fix you, no one will.

Aquarium

A shriek attracts our bored community,
voyeurs ashamed to meet each other's stare.
We rubberneck with bland impunity;

she twists from palsy, pinioned by her chair,
enraged, nurse fluttering for calm in signs
she swats away. We pity her but fear

affliction might undo our own, who line
agape before her misery's display,
ignore the cylinder of aliens

we've paid to witness. Hammerhead and ray,
grouper, eel, pufferfish and needlenose
regard us as if mesmerizing prey.

You tug my hand—a question. She bellows
voicelessly, strains against her muscles' bind,
subsides to weep, exhausted in repose.

"What happened to her, Daddy?" "Never mind."
I hustle you along the spiral walk,
your birth a nightmare gaining from behind:

Entwined by wires within your catafalque,
the NICU nurses' cautious sympathy
through DNR and other paperwork,

the information packet on CP,
the tube through which you'd feed. We reach the lip
and squint across the artificial sea.

Her shriek redoubles, echoing. I grip
the humid rail and mute your hearing aids
against that song until she's made to stop,

then guide you through the granite colonnades,
descend and navigate by exit lights,
red stars releasing us to haven: Day.

Consonance

T

Taste. State. Trees. Street.
Each touch of tongue
tip behind top teeth's
a dance you execute
on point, relax, repeat,
frequency you cannot hear
so roughen into sound,
ungainly muscle jutting pink
through lips pulled down,
fricatives and plosives lisped,
amiss, miscast beyond repair,
syllables elided or abrupt,
incomprehensible to all but
us, patient parent therapists,
our love a pin
you wiggle under, specimen
struck dumb by circumstance
some christen God. *Ta*
we drill the spot
for precious consonants, chisel
past from present tense,
sense from grindstone slur
you rasp into, surrender
ground we struggled for,
to name and own
dividing us from them.
Ta. Ta. Ta. Ta.
Tim tries french fries
twice, three times, again.
Eyes wild you punch
your stone-encumbered mouth,
roar silencing our house—
I CAN'T DO IT—
incisors bared to cut
two lingually accurate t's.

49

S

Your therapist says *s*
frees other consonants—
c, d, l, n, t, z—
tongue quickening with ease,
s from *sh* distinguished,
cicada summer hiss
from shovelful of slush
so words flow smooth and crisp.
Misunderstood, beseeched
to practice joyless speech,
you shape each *cell* and *knee*
excruciatingly.
Lips purse, pull grimace taut,
jaw thrusts to underbite
and locks, breath stops against
thick tongue's impediment.
Somehow, the perfect *s*
arrives, miraculous,
the unexpected guest.
Success. Success. Success.
Suspicious of applause
we'd grant a trained macaw
or chimp, you call the lie:
Do you love me? We shy
away, avoid your praise-
interrogating gaze,
ashamed it's come to this.
Do you love me? Yes. *Yesh?*

R

Round it down, roll to clarify,
narrow, then retract the tongue,
curl sides like wings, a butterfly
your mouth cocoons but cannot free.
Girls are rendered gulls, hard's hod,
the world emerges would,
between what if and then,
this place we've settled in and for.
One-celled syllables subdivide,
bo-re, ca-r, ti-re, ea-r,
never covered properly
so vowels unmoored balloon away.
Are Are Are Are Are Are Are!
I sound like some stupid dog.
We want you to be understood.
I know I'm not like other kids.
We only want what's best for you.
You talk about me like I'm dead.
Our worst misgiving goes unsaid.
(We want you to be one of us.)

Tidying

We poach and bag frayed animals,
familiar guardians of sleep
your mouth drew comfort from. Condemn
disabled toys to charity,
Big Bird's indelicate harangue
deranged by waning batteries.
Cull naked eyeless dolls, a pile
you sift, as if for relatives.
Our mothers bleached, steam-ironed, and snapped
in plastic bins our childhood clothes,
their thrift a mothball redolence
we gag within, so pitch the lot.

You plead to spare one book report,
illuminated cursive manuscript
revised and labored over days,
hot tears winced dry against our rage.
Earnest sentences strategized
to answer who what when where why,
each word inscribed on ruler lines
erased but faintly visible,
title, author, forgotten plot
required to fill a Christmas tree,
curricular absurdity
your thoughtful teachers traced and cut.

"Can't you save anything of me?"
You're pre-nostalgic, canonize
what hasn't vanished yet or fear
what may: We'll steal ourselves away,
a dinner date's convenient lie,
rehearse slow-motion smiles and waves,
compose regretful lullabies
and flee, not looking back, to hide
in states you haven't memorized,
assume elaborate disguise,

hair grown out and dyed, faces pierced
awry, unshaven and unmade,
anonymous on bus or train,
and when confronted by police—
"Are you the parents of?"—deny
we named you in that other world,
choke down the well of love and feign
bemusement with indifferent shrugs:
"Sorry, but—doesn't ring a bell."

Names to Faces, Faces to Names

Have you seen X?
Missing person website,
vigil by candlelight,
their last effects

made souvenirs.
The system's talons stretch,
one's highlighted. Select.
Delete. We fear

the worst and search
no-man's land, abandoned
shed and turnpike island,
a burned-out church

kids party in.
No sign, no goodbye note,
containers emptied out,
door left open,

gone who knows where.
Every livid ember
blackened ash, signatures
becoming air.

The Duettists

The neighbor's grand piano muffled yours,
a stand-up, practical and cheap. Aglow,
hers justified a private studio,
yours the wall between two radiators.

Long fingers bullying worn keys you hurled
"Oklahoma" into Handel minuets,
paused for emphasis, lit a cigarette.
Each coveted the other's secret world,

housewives out for Dionysian blood, rapt
in sheer abandon from the metronome
of meals and tasks and hours, familiar homes
transfiguring wood frames like pods unwrapped

and blown to settle elsewhere, disappear.
Your granddaughter finds yellowed scores and sheets
within the bench, picks out one bar, repeats.
The pedals amplify your echo: *Here.*

The Blister

Late October I ministered your grave
instead of calling home, the phone
an underwater cave

that droned your birthday monotone.
With topsoil, lily bulbs, and garden spade
I thought to cultivate your stone,

no matter being dead
you couldn't notice, would despise
this do-good task, guiltily belated,

an unbeliever's compromise
to till from arid ash
and fragment bone a paradise.

Exhaling steam with every grunt I smashed
thick clay, impossible to cut,
your voice the buried rasp

of tar inhaled, indelicate
laughter hacking reverential silence:
What makes you think I give a shit?

I jammed both feet against
the hasp, burrowing the shovel,
torqued left and right to disengage, then bent

to claw by hand a planting hole.
A damp flame seared my palm;
a blister ripped wept black and full.

Motherf—I stopped myself, abashed to calm,
peeled gingerly the excess crust
and licked it clean, that balm

appeasing your unquiet ghost.
Each pale bulb tamped against marauders' teeth
I said goodbye, my witness lost.

The wound would heal, unsheathe
its carapace to smooth the brand
of skin stretched taut and red, the twinge beneath

your touch, inhabiting my hand.

A Little Old

You'd like to know what happened, right?
Misfortune's cash, exchangeable for pull.
She trembles like a gill-hooked trout;
you feel compelled to say she's beautiful,
not knowing what to say.
You watch through cornered eyes, regret
how summer's passed without the chance to call
tomorrow or today.

She walks, she talks, you'd never know
unless you knew the brain needs oxygen
or else. You gesture, miming "Wow!"
behind her back: God's work. Thy will be done.
We're meant to smile, accept
our modicum of credit due,
bestow upon an audience of one
theatrical respect.

The thing is she's invisible
like us, importunes easily ignored.
We call our pets but can't recall
close neighbors' names or—for that matter—yours,
so fashion similes,
elide embarrassment with smiles,
wave "hi" across the street while doing chores,
observe civilities.

Alone among us, she beheld
the underworld; awoke in wintry air,
first sight on our earth a paneled
ceiling, ensnared by wires to monitors,
and cradled to her chest
this lamb, a sop the hospital
gave infants comatose or DNR.
Having lain unnoticed

hours until the NICU day nurse
came, she devoured one nubbled foot
instead of milk. Tonight, she'll nurse
familiar cloth, stuffed and stitched, nearly shot.
We'd throw the thing away
but picture troubled nights, the worst
fear sleep can conjure hurtling juggernaut
down corridors, a maze

she can't escape, fluorescent glare,
scoured vinegar, red exits dark and cold.
You see her clutching it, inquire
amusedly, "Aren't you a little old?"
She's shamed to realize
her secret's out; now everywhere
she goes your question mocks, a measured scold.
You know you're right: She is.

Luck

Years afterward I find you lost:
Your predatory creditor
for debt no father would forgive,
your midnight dial tone, vengeful ghost
scavenging the household litter.
Hostile witness and detective
I accessed files, newspaper clips,
public records and private tips,
your life's discarded evidence
my hoard, plunder in every word.
Your resume's erased her trail,
colleagues unaware, your penance
silence, confession never heard.
I Google-Earthed your home, surveilled
approaches and escapes in case
misfortune visited, rehearsed
revenge scenarios and worse.
Your route to work became my own,
the bar you haunt, anonymous,
alone, your posture stooped like mine.
Our little secret's burdensome;
we can't escape each other's minds,
lives parallel, her birthday yours,
cruel joke you sought forgiveness for
in calls I dreaded, then ignored.
Remember our post-mortem chat?—
the whys and whens of what you did
or didn't do parsed lawyerlike,
how premiums for birth had spiked.
Cost-effective letting nature
choose which child will breathe, which smother,
observe, discuss, and monitor
but never see or touch—not once—
until you cut, delivered her
stone blue, your hands incarnadined
beyond detergent scrubbing clean.

She's normal, damages controlled;
you'll never hold her dead again.
Her doctors praise rare luck, she's blessed
by medicine, a miracle.
My mind's eye catches yours, and rolls:
No one but us will know unless
I tell. Pursuer and pursued
we stare each other down, afraid
to blink away advantage, lose
the brittle edge we've honed, the blade
for which insurance richly paid
your saving grace, now mine to use.

The Fullness

Assume for now we didn't go along,
observe procedure and indemnify
malpractice, execute the paperwork.

Were hostage to illicit purposes,
swept away by undertow like kittens
drowned and cast downriver, one revenant
clawing from the sack, damaged but intent,
eyes bottomless from having seen too much.

Afraid she'd die, terrified she wouldn't,
we dwelled in ignorance by playing dumb,
conspired against our shared complicity,
knowing what we knew went unacknowledged:
This wasn't what we had in mind at all.

Dismissing circumstantial evidence
we blamed incompetence and managed care,
statistical efficiencies applied
to wring a margin from our bloody mess.

We haven't bargained rights away
or ratted out and abdicated ground
upon whatever cover story's propped
(where you and I house fragile alibis).

For now amnesia envelops us,
a current slow enough to hasten sleep
so what we didn't do or should have done
recedes, incriminating documents
erase themselves, forgive as we forget.

Suppose we're old together and avoid
each other's eyes, ashamed, our secret safe
inside the silence pooling every space
and hollowing what's left of us, until
we're nothing less than full, and nothing more?

To a Peanut

Misnomered bean of many purposes,
spreadable or whole, Carver's humble muse,

you lurk between ingredients as oil,
a manufacture trace enough to swell

pale lips to crimson plates and supersize
her tongue until she suffocates and dies.

I govern daughters rivalrous as queens,
one deaf from birth, her younger sister keen

with jealousy for unshared attention.
My routine weekend blur of errands runs

a slide show of suburban photo ops,
from dump to dry cleaner to Stop 'n Shop

where, goading me, she chews you by mistake,
collapsing in anaphylactic shock

I can't arrest—her Epi-pen at home,
forgotten there with Benadryl and phone—

nor press a key to pause indifferent time,
excuse the blame or craft an alibi,

release her throat from inflammation's grip
to breathe and shriek, again an infant ripped

into our world. Imagining such harm
I grimace through a smile as she performs,

displaying you as if the universe
between two fingertips, creation hers,

blue eyes aglow with self-important glee:
"Now *I* can have a disability!"

Graduation

The third or fifth in any company
she lingers with a moist, too-eager nose,
eyes desperate, the artificial grin
I've guaranteed will open doors stretched taut.
Encircled girls regard her as disease,
toss curtained hair and quarter-turn away,
lift slim shoulders, glance among themselves, smile
so knowingly I'm rendered impotent
with rage. She wanders counterclockwise, shunned.
I could intrude, broker conversation,
mime other fathers' cheerful quips but don't,
determined she negotiate a way
between her difference to theirs, and mine.

Ten years of therapy produced today,
case-managed, mainstreamed, base objectives met,
unburdened from the stations of her cross—
fine motor, balance, auditory, speech—
the same regime her grandmother endured
post-op, recovering from strokes. She's rare,
a brutal rule's exception and its proof:
The brain craves oxygen and suffocates
unnecessary nerves to save itself.
Her files encompass yards of cabinet.
There can't be what, one hundred worldwide? Ten?
Or she alone, arrayed invisible
in normal guise, posing yes/no questions
to elicit dialogue, hearing aids
beneath a scrunchie band the giveaway.

I witness with their calculating gaze,
these girls, teeth braced against unsightly drift,
heads cocked in minute unison to mark
this special alien—slurred consonants,
voice rough as if exhaled through clotted earth,
a traveler from blackened realms who seeks
companionship and hastens for that fire,
above which native speakers perch
in shadow, parsing her non sequitur:
"Remember when we toasted marshmallows?"

Lift Every Voice

Released
the signal roams
directionless   between
unneighborly colonials
shades drawn against hard February glare
lawns clenched   immaculate with frost
no listener until
it enters here
fine labyrinth of wire
implanted on her shaven skull
and threaded through the tender middle ear
where cilia and ossicle
frail handmaidens of sound
no longer serve
excised by surgery
electrodes in precise array
transmitting digital approximates
along the auditory nerves
0 1 0 1
a code her brain
reconstitutes as song's
familiar miracle   two tones
inquire expectantly   one long   one short
she startles out "What's that?" and turns
discovering the wren
within its oak
head cocked to double check
behind   around   above   below
where she stands rapt   agape as if possessed
her quickened gaze a gift the bird
escapes with flight   too keen
to bear   too dear
to keep

The Black Parade

We shuffle through the mortuary hall,
visitors cordoned right, departures left,
acknowledging with grimaces and nods.
Our destination's open for respects,

spouse poised to hear each well-meant homily
and comfort those who can't control themselves.
The perfectly embalmed facsimile
half-smiles, amused at one remove, a shell

scraped clean and polished with emollients,
all ravages erased. Some mourners kneel
before the casket, others look askance,
unsettled by her forfeit privacy.

The daughter and her grade school friends defile
the quiet rooms, rude birds arrayed to feed,
exclaiming at each other's brazen hues,
our gravity a plain they sport above

as on this canvas, lacquered dim and crazed
with age, a laden cart from home to home
proceeds along the filthy central way
toward hills beyond the shuttered town, up which

more carts approach a smudge suggesting flame,
accompanied by ashen supplicants,
palms raised, faces lit with fear or shame,
and one detail that draws the viewer close:

A girl cavorts behind the black parade,
old initiate, eager eyes aglow,
the cart, the town, the crematory hills,
the whole perspective narrowing to her.

67

Blueberries

My breakfast brims with antioxidants.
Another free-trade coffee for the road.
These wheat squares qualify as penitence,

radicals defeated, all systems run.
I spoon down mouthfuls, sharply sweet; a nerve
ignites my tongue where you return, undone,

each CAT-scanned bone and organ colonized.
You will not eat, sustained by oxygen,
crave nothing but to smoke again. Dad sighs

and disconnects the hissing tank to strike
a match. Doug raids Whole Foods for blueberries,
green labeled locavore organic milk,

ingredients he whips into a blend.
Sue tilts the straw, entreating you to try.
Contrite, agreeable, you make amends

for us and suck, grown children meaning well—
thick foam congealed with shredded pulps of skin—
then gag, your stomach-turning groan a knell,

apologize for being such a bore.
I wipe your spittled mouth while wiping mine,
lips blue, teeth dull with grain, and swallow more.

One Last Thing

I wasn't always half-ass paralyzed.
My forehand made you flinch at net, head-high
   or hammered in your balls: Don't poach.
Who swam down strangers' panicked kids adrift
   in tide, defused the humming hive,
   cooked, cleaned, sanded, raked, planted, coached,
decapitated snakes before they bit?

Guess who. Now I'm eclipsed by passing news.
Each year consumes another friend who knew
   me when, before strokes fried me white:
Bleached hair, pronged cane, a witch because undrowned.
   I'm done, irrelevant, amuse
   those so inclined or impolite
enough to feign delight I'm still around,

gossip stirred with bile, seasoned to malign.
I've learned to listen rather than opine.
   You're big on lending expertise;
men imagine we can't handle pressure,
   establish status quo aligned
   with jokes, dismissives aimed to please,
whatever shuts us up or self-assures.

My kitchen doubled as confessional
for neighbors under house arrest, tongues held,
   bread buttered, tiny slippers clasped.
The things I heard would curl your thinning hair.
   Perfect lives of perfect people
   often aren't; tears and snot collapse
foundations, liner runneled past repair.

"Oh Eva, don't you ever want to…" What,
vacation in some b.s. Camelot?
   Like Jackie O they stockpiled shoes,
accumulated clothes against decay,

clipped tips for blowing ashes hot.
　Each strand of pearls became a noose
they couldn't loosen over chardonnay,

kept very well by mutual consent
while pawning jewelry to cover rent.
　They bitched without alternatives,
no context. Once, fed up and furious,
　　rearguing an argument
　　I planned imaginary drives
away to Denver and my parents' house

which wasn't there, and Rose and Joe long gone,
our neighborhood paved over and rezoned.
　Idling downtown, the Pontiac's
Ahem good company, I cried until
　　this cop inquired: Was I alone,
　　did I need help or know to ask?
Humiliated stiff, I bared a smile,

displaying lipsticked teeth as camouflage.
His pity made me bite my lip in rage.
　Returning home, I didn't trust
my temper so proceeded with routine,
　　tasks prioritized by triage,
　　floor swept, counters wiped, table bussed.
My little misadventure went unseen

but that cop's questions cut me near the bone.
Don't let another notice you alone.
　You're rendered an anomaly,
the least mistake confines you in the ditch.
　　Your disability's disowned:
　　Good luck. The happy homilies
sewn for display unravel, lies from stitch

to seam. Commercial sympathy absolves
the sender of providing help, or love.
    A card enforces etiquette.
I've seen eyes drop, received the gracious kiss
    that greets and razors objects of
    compassion. Tit for tat, get it?
If poetry's your version of noblesse

oblige, don't bother resurrecting me.
I'd just as soon lie low in memory
    between stray details and to-do's,
forgettable, unearthed by accident.
    Ends can be my emissary:
    Warped Kramer racquet, garden tools,
a whelk, the hive, a wing's eroded tent,

the pall of someone lighting cigarettes
inside despite explicit rules, regrets
    a *fuck you* under breath. I'll be
available, though you won't recognize
    my disembodied voice unless
    it echoes unexpectedly.
I won't invade familiar lullabies.

I'll find another entryway. Surprise.

The Defender

He dribbles out, this skinny boy.
His feet perform magician's sleight:
Roll and stop, stutter-step, create
havoc as midfielders deploy,

give chase but fall away, too late.
Adept, precise beyond nine years
outdistancing his lumpen peers
he measures the triumvirate

of fullbacks, angles left, then veers
abruptly in, is overrun
by two who sag, deceived again.
Opposing sideline parents cheer;

there's one defender still: Helen.
This boy has no idea how hard
she's run, how willingly, how far.
Delivered blue, no oxygen

until revived by CPR
she slept ten silent days, near dead,
surrendered to machines and fed
through tubes, refused to thrive, Apgar

scores sequentially encoded
toward an end that never came.
Across black ice we called her name;
she woke within the NICU bed

becalmed, ghost ship arriving home.
Wound tight, unable to relax
she ran awry, head twisted back
appraising where she'd been, caromed

into trees, charged through glass. Attacks
red-faced, breath audible in gasps,
hair wild, one hearing aid unclasped
and dangling, uniform amok,

disheveled maenad closing fast.
When they collide the sound rebounds,
bone ringing bone. He buckles down
slow motion, perfect limbs a masque

of aspiration brought to ground.
It isn't fair. The ball spurts free.
She staggers forward gracelessly,
collects herself, and clears the zone

upfield, escaping memory,
oblivious to whistles' blare,
never mind the boy whose father
howls in torment. The referee

arrives and into October's
limpid sky unfurls a yellow
flag, redistributing its glow,
light brimming everywhere, for her.

About the Author

George Witte is the author of two previous collections, *Deniability* and *The Apparitioners*. His poems have been published in numerous journals, and reprinted in the *Best American Poets 2007, Vocabula 2, Old Flame,* and *Rabbit Ears* anthologies. He received the Frederick Bock Prize from *Poetry* magazine and a fellowship from the New Jersey State Council on the Arts. For twenty-nine years he has worked at St. Martin's Press, where he is editor-in-chief. He lives with his wife and their two daughters in Ridgewood, New Jersey.

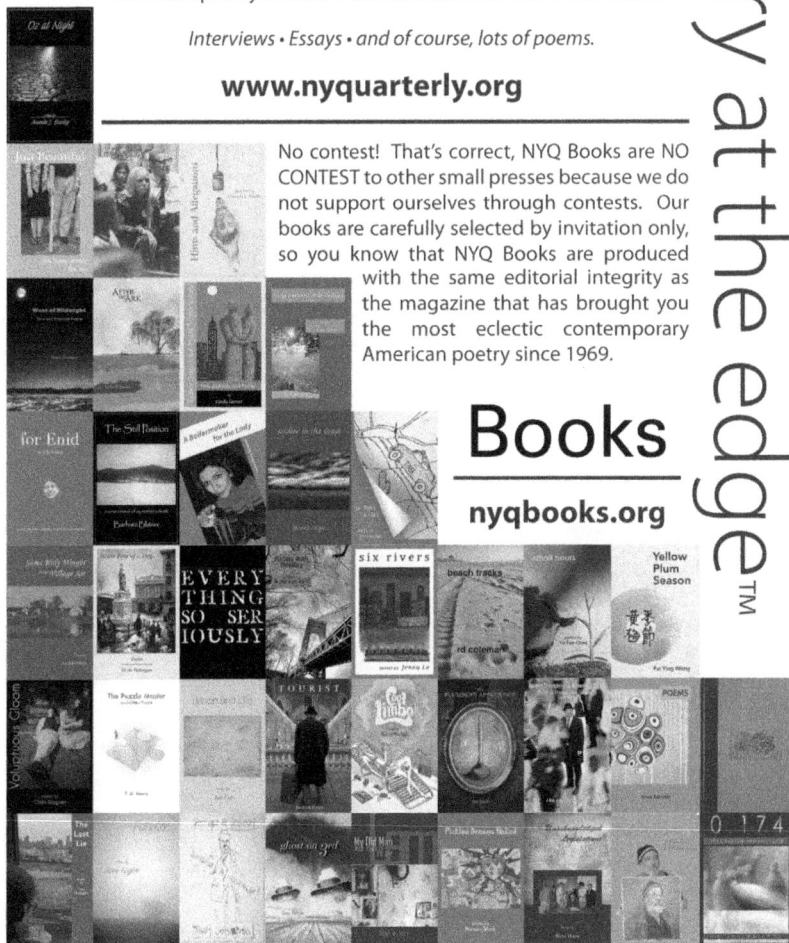

www.ingramcontent.com/pod-product-compliance
Lightning Source LLC
LaVergne TN
LVHW091231080426
835509LV00009B/1240